How To Become A Millionaire
Buying & Selling
Properties
In ThaHood

The advice and strategies contained herein may not be suitable for your situation. You should consult with a professional where appropriate. Neither the publisher nor the author shall be liable for any lose of profit or any other commercial damages.

Follow me on Twitter @Mr7figga

HOW TO BECOME A MILLIONAIRE BUYING & RENTING PROPERTIES
IN THE HOOD

HOW TO BECOME A MILLIONAIRE BUYING & RENTING PROPERTIES
IN THA HOOD

A BOOK BY: POE

This book is dedicated to the memory of my Father who always wanted to be in the Real Estate Business

The secret to success is: Desire, Ambition, Motivation, and not to get left sitting in the "Waiting Room" FLOYD SIMMS

ACKNOWLEDGMENTS

I would like to first thank my Wife (a real top soldier) who has been down with me through the good and many bad times; I would also like to thank my Sister "Valerie" who has always believed in and supported me from the very beginning; and to my Real Estate Agent ("Denise Brown"). I have to say thank you. You're the best!! Without Denise guiding me through the early stages of my real estate investing I don't think I would've made it in this business.

TABLE OF CONTENTS

INTRODUCTION

I have never considered myself to be a writer and I certainly never considered myself as someone who would sit down and write an entire book, but almost everyday I have different people calling me, texting me, or emailing me, just to ask me how they too can make money as I have from investing in cheap real estate that's located in "Tha Hood". People just can't understand how I do it? What's my secret to making money in a downward real estate cycle where houses aren't selling anymore?

Well, I'll tell you this. If you pay cash for an investment property and have a positive cash flow, market pricing cycles don't matter. The long term "buy and hold" approach is always going to be based on the properties ability to create cash flow. The fast resale approach is not going to happen again any time soon. I'd say not for at least another six or seven years, but at least you can be assured that in the long run your property will eventually appreciate again.

It's no secret that some of the most money to be made is in tha hood (Ghetto). Just look at all the drug dealer's driving around in their fancy cars and living in those big houses after they've made tons of money standing out on the comer all day selling drugs. Look at the Arabs who come over from the middle east and opens up stores on every comer that's available. Look at all the Liquor Stores. Most of them are all located

in the Inner Cities. Then look at the Pimps who sells Women, and the illegal gambling dens, and the Booster's who sells stolen clothes at a huge discount. It's estimated that more than $1 billion dollars flows in and out of the American Ghetto's each year, and that the biggest money maker of them all is not from the sell of drugs or alcohol but from the rents collected from real estate.

Around 2008-2009 when the housing market crashed a lot of homes in the poor communities were left abandoned and this in turned left the banks holding onto a lot of properties that they didn't need or want. So in order to get rid of millions of these foreclosed or abandoned homes across America the banks decided to sell of these properties for almost pennies on the dollar.

During this same time not only has the United States had to deal with it's own high rate of homelessness but it is also experiencing a huge influx of new citizens coming in from other countries such as Mexico, Africa, and Asia. When these people arrive in the United States they need emergency assistance and shelter or housing. So the United States has to place them in homes or apartments through their Section 8 Programs. This is where I come in... I'm a real estate investor who's also an opportunist. I know that the government has money set aside for their Section 8 Programs. I also know that if I have a home that can pass a simple health and safety inspection the government will pay me good money if I allow one of their Section 8 participants to live in one of my investment properties.

Although the housing bubble that was so huge a few years ago has fmally busted, it is still a very good time to buy real estate, and the best properties to acquire are the one's in tha hood. In area's where nobody else will go and also where you can buy houses and apartment buildings for under $20,000; fix them up and then rent them out to people on government assistance.

I'm successful in this business simply because I figured out a way to make a lot of money by buying these ran down homes that nobody else would touch. The fact is that most ran down bank owned houses in tha hood are really not that bad. Most of these houses only need very little cosmetic work.

Choosing the correct property would be to choose one that earns long-term profits. Right now, the best properties to purchase as investments are the one's in tha hood that's totally beat up, ran down, and dilapidated with no windows, plumbing, etc. The one's that no one else will even consider purchasing. Even if you pay $10,000 for the property and have to put in another $5,000-$7,000 to do repairs. You're still going to come out ahead of the game because you've still spent way below market value and at the same time you've created some positive cash flow once it's rented out.

Now, the best way to achieve positive cash flow is to purchase cheap bank owned properties (with cash) and fix them up, thereby increasing the value of the property. Area's with lower home prices are more likely to have positive cash flow because in tha hood there is a much higher demand for rentals because not a lot of people own their own homes.

Cash flow refers to the amount of cash coming in relative to the amount going out. Since you're going to be paying cash for the home all you'll have to do is deduct your rental property's monthly insurance, property taxes, and utilities. (If you have the property rented out, then the tenant should be paying all the utilities) Once you calculate these few expenses you'll subtract them from your monthly rent. Anything left over would be considered positive cash flow, and also a good indicator that the property is a valuable asset.

Look, I'm proof that this system works. Today, I have 29 rental properties valued at $1,700,000 and I collect rents from 25 of those each month. Not all of these rents are the same but on average I collect about $700.00 from each of them. That's $17,500 a month positive cash flow. Times that by twelve and I'm getting $210,000 a year! And this is all being paid to me by the United States Government's Section 8 Program.

Talk about living the American Dream. I am that dream, and I'm writing this book to show you all that you too can be living that dream. I guarantee that after reading this book you will have no problem creating wealth through those properties in tha hood that no one else will touch. So read on and I hope you enjoy this book.

WAIT...DON'T QUIT YOUR DAY JOB

Before you continue reading this book, I would like to make one thing clear. I am not a fan of anyone quitting their day job to start working full time as a real estate investor.

A lot of people think that investing in real estate will instantly make them rich overnight. Well, it's very easy to get caught up in the "flip this house" hype that you read about or watch on television. Certainly, you can make a lot of money in the real estate business but it takes time. First, you are going to need to diligently research and learn as much as you can about the real estate business, then you must develop your business into a stable , steady, stream of income that you can rely on before calling it quits with your regular 9-5 job.

Also, you must be sure that real estate is something that you really want to do. You must have a passion for it, and if you don't already have a passion for it you'd better develop one real soon.

I started doing real estate on the side while I was still fully employed many years ago, and I didn't quit my steady job until my properties were generating more money than I was making at my real job.

I am not trying in any way to scare anyone away from investing in the real estate business. Obviously, if I were I wouldn't be writing this book. I just want the reader to understand that there are certain things you'll need to think about before you decide to take such a big risk, because once you quit your day job you must be ready to start working even harder than you did with your regular 9-5 job. Additionally, be realistic. It may take possibly 3-5 years or more before you start to see any real significant amount of cash flow, and for the average man or woman with a family, bills, and a mortgage to pay each month this business can not only be stressful but also unpleasant.

Remember, it takes money to make money so with that said you'll need to already have some money saved and ready to invest. Again, you may not be able to recoup this money for several years.

Chasing a dream isn't for everyone. Being a Real Estate Tycoon is something I've wanted to be all my life. As a child monopoly was my favorite game to play and it still is today. However, not everyone thinks like I do. Some people would rather have stability and the security of a regular 9-5 job to go to each day. Some of us just don't like to take risk and that's okay but for those of us who doesn't mind taking risk real estate investing might be for you. But, remember, before you take the real estate investor's leap you'll need to educate yourself on the basics of real estate in general. Go to your local library and read up on all the real estate investment books written by professionals with experience in this field. You're going to need to have some understanding of how real estate transactions work and what real estate investor's do to create positive cash flow.

It should be noted here that being a real estate investor is not the same as being a real estate agent. There is a big difference between the two. Real Estate Agents go out and find properties for the buyer or investor and makes a commission for doing so. Very easy, right? Whereas, the Real Estate Investor's job is much more difficult because the Investor has to buy the property, then spend more money to hire contractor's to rehab the property, watch over the contractor's to make sure they're doing their jobs correctly, then once it's fmished the Investor has to advertise and market the property to rent or sell. Not that easy!

I've known several people who has used their life savings or dipped into their "40lk plan" an entered into the world of real estate investing just to lose it all a few years later because they didn't know what they were doing. These individuals did not take the time to learn and understand how this business works. Sure, it's easy to look at "Donald Trump", "R. Donahue Peebles", "Jorge Perez", or "H. Roger Neal" and see all their success from real estate investing
but neither of them became rich overnight. It took them years of hard

work before they became independently wealthy and could rely solely on their steady stream of income from their real estate investment's before they could quit their day jobs.

With that said I hope the reader will enjoy reading the rest of this book and perhaps learn from my experiences as a successful real estate investor who has became a millionaire buying and renting properties in tha hood.

HOW TO FIND A GOOD REAL ESTATE AGENT

There's a difference between a Realtor and a Real Estate Agent. All Realtors are licensed to sell real estate as an agent or broker but not all real estate agents are realtors. To be a Realtor you must be a member of the National Association of Realtors. This requires that agents take additional training above the licensing requirements.

Finding a good Real Estate Agent is about the most important thing you will need to do when starting out in the real estate investment business. You will need to fmd an agent that specializes in foreclosures or bank owned properties. A good agent doesn't necessarily work at a big real estate company or sell the most houses or even make a lot of money. A good agent is one who is experienced and knows the market that you wish to invest in.

Randomly looking in the phone book and just picking a name is not going to be enough. You should ask family, friends, neighbors, and co-worker's if they can refer you to a good agent. Most Real Estate Agent's come by referrals, and successful Agents will satisfy their clients needs so try to fmd an Agent who will go far beyond his/her responsibilities to fmd you a great property and get you a good deal as well.

If I were just starting out in the real estate investing business I would perhaps first try the internet and try googling "the top Realtor's who specializes in bank owned or foreclosed properties". You might also want to think about trying an Agent who's new to the business because they may be a little hungrier and much more willing to spend more time looking for that first deal. Essentially, the two of you can get started in the business together.

Another good way to fmd a good Real Estate Agent may be to just drive around a particular area that you're interested in and look for Signs in the front yards of houses that are for sale. You'll want to call three or four of these agent's to see not who has the most properties listed "For Sale" but who's listings are selling the fastest. Most likely the Agent who's selling houses the fastest has put in place a better advertising and marketing strategy.

If you know of any Handyman, Contractor's, or Mortgage Representatives, these people will most likely know someone that they can recommend to you.

When you do find that one agent that you believe will be essential to helping you accomplish your goal of becoming a millionaire in tha hood. Make sure you see how he/she operates. Is the Agent savvy with the web? How much does he/she know about advertising and marketing a property? Can he/she guide you through the entire process of buying, selling, or even closing on a house? See if they can even explain to you what a fmal HUD page is? Also, see if your new Agent can recommend to you service provider's such as Roofer's, Carpenter's, Painter's, Carpet Installer's, Tile Layer's, etc, etc...and ask your Agent questions about how he/she will price the house if you buy and then decide to re-sale. You should know that supply and demand in a particular neighborhood will play a big role in how your Agent has to price the property. Keep the big picture in mind and try not to get overly emotionally involved or attached to any specific property.

Finally, your Real Estate Agent is suppose to work with you to take the buying and selling of your properties easier.

REGISTERING YOUR COMPANY'S NAME

For legal reasons you may want to think about registering your company's name and forming some kind of Corporation or Limited Liability Company (L.L.C.). My Company's legal name is: "Capital One Realty And Property Management L.L.C. I named it this because I am from the Capital City of Ohio which is also the largest City in Ohio which makes it the number one City also, thus, the name.

A very good reason why you should think about registering your business is to protect yourself from any lawsuits that may arise in the future. Such as: Someone slipping on ice in front of your building, a tenant getting injured inside your property, or even if someone tries to sue you for something your tenant has done to them. If for whatever reason you are ever successfully sued the person suing you can only sue your Company and not you personally. It is the Corporation not you who will be sued.

Finally, you should register your business and it's name just so that you and someone else won't be using the same name. It would be very confusing for you both, and you'll both probably end up mistakenly taking business from each other.

So, all you have to do in order to register your business is go to the web site of your states' "Secretary of State". Once you're on the site you can then search to see if there's any other business using your name or a similar name. If no one else is using the name you've selected, you can register the name following whatever directions the Secretary of State gives you.

CASH IS KING

When buying that first investment property I would strongly advise the investor to pay with cash. Why? Well, the reasons are simple:

1) The luxury of no monthly mortgage payment.

2) Buying with cash eliminates Mortgage interest.

3) The cash buyer doesn't spend money, time, or effort obtaining a loan.

4) Cash buyer's don't have to obtain a property appraisal.

5) Cash gives the buyer greater purchasing power. Having all cash makes negotiating a dis≠ count a strong probability.

6) The cash buyer can take out a loan later, using the homes value as collateral.

But, before you can get started on your journey to becoming a successful real estate investor you have to make sure that your own fmances are in a healthy enough state that you can wait for the property to start producing cash flow. True real estate investing doesn't start with buying rental property, it begins with creating the fmancial situation where you can buy a rental property.

With property values in low income neighborhoods being at their lowest point since the early 1980's, cash deals are a lot easier to negotiate and bank owned properties are even easier. Banks are not in the real estate business, nor do they want to be. Banks are in the business of loaning money and charging interest in order to make a profit. Banks don't want properties sitting in their portfolio costing them money to maintain. Bad loans (called nonperforming loans because they pay no interest) are what the banks don't want. When bank owned properties are sitting vacant the banks have to hire a Property

Preservation Company to take care of those properties, so if you have a seasoned Real Estate Agent she can probably negotiate a good deal for you. But, when buying investment properties it's always best to begin with the end in mind. Your only reason for buying investment properties should be to generate cash flow. You should also have some sort of guidelines along with a time frame to reach your objective. Don't forget you must be patient and cautious as an investor, and buy only when you know the deal is a good one.

I personally like paying cash for these cheap properties because I can take my time fixing them up. There's no mortgage so I don't have to worry about rushing to get the property together in order to get it rented, in order to pay the bank their monthly note. No, I don't want anyone breathing down my neck hounding me for money. And, once I have a property fixed up I try to only rent to Section 8 Tenant's. (I will explain my reasons for doing this in a later chapter) I also put a portion of my monthly rents away for yearly taxes, and the rest I save in order to invest in more properties.

After the housing market crashed in most of the United States. Housing prices have dropped ten times from what they were 10-15 years ago. In some parts of the country such as: Miami, Phoenix, Buffalo, Detroit, Atlanta, Cleveland and Columbus, Ohio; buyer's can fmd bank owned foreclosures for well under $20,000. I myself have purchased dozens of homes for less than $10,000. Right now, banks are desperate to sell these houses and when there's desperation, there's opportunity. I like to buy properties in mid-western states that are priced below $10,000 and needs little repair. If you look hard enough you can find a house that needs less than $5,000 in repairs. Trust me they're out there. You just have to look.

These homes typically offer better overall return from the rental income you'll collect. Remember, even in a bad market rental prices will hold steady.

For the beginning investor, I would advise them to focus only in their local market and to get to know that market as well as they can and because you will focus on renting to individuals who have a Section 8 Certificate it will be important to be as close to Schools, Hospitals, Fire, and Police Stations as possible for safety reasons.

By low, rent high. Buying the right investment properties will give you the ability to create cash flow. Most people overlook cash flow when it comes to investing in real estate. This is because most real estate investor's lack fmancial education when it comes to buying investment properties. Generally, it's harder to accurately predict cash flow than it is to predict capital gain. So in order to make the rent pay, you have to have a formula for evaluating rental income. Here's mine: Rent+2/Price=yield

Rent: Divide annual rental income in half to account for the cost of vacancies.

Price: The full price you paid for the property including closing cost.

Yield: The return on your investment. In todays market I look for 5 to 7 percent.

Note: This formula works best for properties worth less than $20,000

Personally speaking, I don't see any reason why more people are not rich. "John D. Rockefeller" once said that...."As an American Citizen, it's your duty to be rich!" I would like to think that he meant everyone. It doesn't matter if you're black, white, red, or brown.

The disaster from the housing market crash is nothing but an opportunity for more people to create wealth. If you're now living in "tha hood" and everyday you walk down the street, you see people who don't live in your hood buying houses, fixing them up, and renting them out for a profit, you're not doing your duty as an American Citizen. Do not look at these houses as eye sores. Look at them as opportunities. I see people from other countries come to the United States and create wealth from nothing more than the desire to have more. Those people are all living the American Dream.

While writing this book I can reflect back on when I purchased my first property. At the time I was working for the "Coca Cola Company" and my job was to drive around the city and check different stores to see if they were fully stocked with our product. As I drove around some of the inner city area's (tha hood) I would often look at all the abandoned houses and wonder to myself "why doesn't the city just tear those properties down?" They were abandoned, dilapidated, and falling apart. A real bad eye sore. Well, one day my Sister just called me out of the blue telling me about and investment idea she had. (Now, I want the reader to remember that this was at the height of the housing boom) She told me that she had been watching television and came across a program talking about the real estate boom and how people from all over the country were getting rich by flipping houses. She wanted to know if I would be willing to go in half with her to purchase a cheap property? Well, since I was in a dead in job anyway and wasn't making much money I decided to take that leap of faith and inter into the real estate investment business. The only problem on my end was that I didn't have much money to start with. I told her to give me a few weeks to see if I could come up with a little extra money.

She started looking for properties and soon found a two-unit duplex that had a asking price of $31,500. She had her half of the money. I needed mine. I had managed to save about $3,500 in the bank and I also had pretty good credit but I didn't want to take out a loan if I didn't have to. So, what I did was called creative fmancing. I had an insurance policy that I could borrow from and an old antique guitar that I knew I could pawn. Altogether I came up with $11,500 and my Sister allowed me to owe her the rest. This is how I purchased my first property. We went to the seller's with all cash and closed on the property in less than 30 days. After doing some minor repairs we were able to quickly rent out the two units. Unfortunately, soon after my Sister decided she didn't like being in the real estate business and later sold me her half of the property.(Remember, earlier I talked about having a passion for this business. Well, my Sister realized that she just didn't have the time or energy to devote herself to real estate investing) Almost three years later I sold that same property for $90,000 and doubled my investment.

This is why I strongly advise anyone wanting to get into the real estate business not to quit their day job, if they already have one. Because you do not get rich over night. It takes years of hard work and investing. I'm simply sharing my experience with the readers to show you how real estate can help you take control of your financial future. If you want to acquire wealth, and become financially independent it's best to follow the lead of people who are already successful. Most millionaires in the United States derive their wealth from real estate. That's why I would recommend real estate over any other investment. Remember, if you want to be successful do what successful people do.

I have another example of why cash is king. A few years back I came across another duplex located on the near east side of Columbus, Ohio. It was a bank owned foreclosure and the asking price was $36,000. I drove over to take a look at this property and I must say, it was in terrible shape. The kitchens and bathrooms had been totally destroyed, the plumbing and electrict wiring were missing, and the stairs leading down into the basement were gone. This place needed a total rehab done on it, but I saw that it had tremendous potential. I gave my real estate agent a call and told her exactly what I had seen and asked her if there was anyway we could negotiate the price down. She called me later that day and informed me that there had already been several full price offer's made on the property. I instructed her to call the bank back and explain to them that I would pay all cash if the bank would be willing to come down on their asking price. I offered them $28,000. The cash offer did the trick because the very next day my agent called and told me that the bank had indeed accepted my offer.

They accepted my offer simply because it was cash. The bank did not want to waste anymore time holding onto this property that was costing them money daily.

I closed on the property and immediately gutted it down to the studs.

I did a lot of the work myself to save money. I re-did the kitchens and bathrooms, put in new windows and doors, and installed new stairs leading down into the basement. After spending a total of $13,000; I was able to bring the Units back to almost new. I rented both Units out and a year and a half later I sold the duplex for $66,000. Making a very nice $25,000 profit.

The fact is, cash will get you started on your road to success a lot faster than going to the bank asking for a line of credit.

CHOOSING YOUR FIRST PROPERTY
That Diamond In The Rough

Personally, I never waste my time driving around aimlessly looking for homes to buy. That's what I have a Real Estate Agent for. With today's internet highway being full of information my agent can fmd houses for me and then forward them to me by email. Each morning when I arrive at my Office there's already hundreds of properties for me to look at. If I see one that I might be interested in, only then, will I drive by to look at it. If you're already living in "tha hood" you might want to try and fmd something around your area. This way you will be close to your property. You can also manage it better and if something goes wrong you won't have to drive across town to check on it.

Searching for your first investment property may seem like a lot of work. It may even become a little bit overwhelming and a bit stressful at first, but don't give up. Be realistic, remember, this is "tha hood" and all you want is a decent property that can make you some extra income.

It's really up to you if you want your first investment property to be a Single Family Home, a Duplex, or a Multi-Unit dwelling with 3 or more Units. I, personally, prefer single family homes because they're easier to manage. Single Family Homes tend to attract long term Tenant's. If you have a Family of say, three or more, they tend to not be as likely to move out after a one year lease is up. Reason being, it's a lot harder for an entire Family to up and move out than it is for a single person living in a apartment.

When looking for your first investment property you should try to take notes and focus on what really matters. Don't worry about small things that can be easily fixed or repaired such as paint, countertops, and floor tiles. You should instead concentrate on the big stuff, such as the roof and structural issues. Although you're in "tha hood" you'll want to try and fmd properties that may still have a furnace, water heater, plumbing, and electrical wiring. Because these items will cost you the most if they're not already in the property.

Also, try not to worry about appreciation or what other properties have sold for in the neighborhood. Remember, you're not planning to sell your investment property for several years. At least, not while the real estate market is down. You only want to rent the property out, and for appreciation potential, you only want to do a few cosmetic changes and renovations. This alone will raise the properties value in case you do want to sell when the market has come back up.

Due diligence plays a big role in me deciding if I might want to put in an offer on a property or not. If you've never brought a property before I would strongly suggest that you $350.00 and hire a professional home inspector to go through the house and tell you exactly what's wrong with it. Fortunately for me, after buying and re≠ habbing more than a hundred investment properties I kinda have an idea what to look for when I walk through a potential property. It is also very important to make sure the property has no liens against it. Before closing, make sure a Title search has been done and ask for Title Insurance. This way if the Title company misses something you will be protected.

While on your search to fmd that first investment property you will probably come across several Multi-Units. Only you can decide if owning and managing a Multi-Unit Building is right for you. The taxes will certainly be higher and so will the maintenance fees, but you'll also be collecting alot more rent. If you can fmd a four-unit building in decent shape and it doesn't need a lot of work done to it in order to bring it back to life, I would say go for it. I have several four-unit's in my portfolio that I own and they each generate a positive cash flow for me each month. However, the turn over in Tenant's are a lot higher. Some tenant's are late with their rent each month and some don't pay at all. This is when you'll start the eviction proceedings, which I will discuss in a later chapter. On average, I will lose a tenant from each of my buildings once every four months.

If four-unit's are what you really want to invest in I can give you a basic estimate of what you can expect to make monthly free and clear. Let's say you charge $500 a month per unit times four. That's $2000. Now, minus general maintenance cost (grass-cutting, snow removal, building utilities, and other miscellaneous) $250 plus, property taxes $250.00(monthly). You'll walk away with about $1500 each month. However, you cannot always expect 100% occupancy so you should deduct another $500. This will leave you with $1000 month in rental income. CASH FLOW. You will want to always try and position yourself to make money.

A few examples of advantages of owning a multi- unit is: cash flow, equity capture, leverage, and appreciation.

Cash Flow: is what I just described to you above. It's the profit you make after all the expenses have been deducted.

Equity Capture: is when you can seize added value at the time of purchase. Example: if you fmd a four- unit that has appraised for $150,000 but you purchase it for only $30,000. This creates instant equity in the amount of $120,000 that can be obtained at the time you sale.

Leverage: is when you can borrow against the property by assuming less exposure to the loss of your own property.

Appreciation: let's assume that you buy a four unit for $30,000 and hold onto it 10 years, and over the course of those 10 years, the value of the property goes up to $150,000. It has risen in value.

You've heard the saying "one man's junk is another man's treasure". This is true when it comes to those ugly ass, ran down, houses that are in tha hood. Most investors try to avoid properties that are in disarray or needs considerable repairs done on them. However, the smart investors look specifically for these types of properties because they know that there's a mountain of profits to be made with a monthly cash flow commgm.

The fact is that most ran down, bank owned, houses in tha hood are really not that bad. Most of these houses only need very little cosmetic work. Even if you pay $10,000 and do another $5000 in repairs you're still spending way below market value if you're renting it out as an investment property and you charge let's say $500 a month. You will make your entire investment back in 2 lh years. Not bad. And, should you decide to sell it after 2 lh years you will have made a profit and your money back.

If you're going to buy a ran down home in tha hood at least try to fmd one that only looks like it needs a lot of work. This can be a good negotiating tool with the bank. Most likely the bank who owns the property has not actually went out and physically viewed the property. They are probably 1000 miles a way sitting in an office hoping someone will just take the property of their hands. What has happened is the bank has hired a real estate agent who deals specifically with bank owned properties, and that agent has hired a property preservation company to go out and take pictures of the place and access the condition of the property. Thereafter, sending photos and a condition report back to the agent who forwards copies onto the bank. By looking at those pictures a lot of times the bank (and agents) will value the property at the very low end of what other comparable's (comps) are in the area . So, if the house is located in the ghetto it most likely will be listed reasonably cheap. I recently purchased a house in not so bad of an area of tha hood for $6899 and all it needed were new kitchen cabinets and fresh paint on the walls. It was in such good shape that it passed Section 8 inspection and they granted my request for rent which was $700 a month. I will make my investment back in a year. I love tha hood!!

Donald Trump once said.." Live where you want, but invest where it makes sense." So choosing the correct property would be to choose one that earns long-term profits.

MAKING THE RIGHT OFFER

So you've found the perfect investment property. Now, all you need to do is make an offer and close the deal. As I stated earlier, banks are not in the real estate business nor do they want to be, and they certainly don't want to be out in the streets peddling houses. But, never mistake a bank owned/foreclosure as a sign of desperation. The banks are not all the way desperate. They may have marked the house down (if it's in tha hood) way below market value but just because it's a piece of crap doesn't mean they're going to just give it to you.

Over the past 10 years I have successfully negotiated multiple bank owned deals. Banks never want to be insulted. Especially, after they've already had to foreclose and take back a home. So just because a house is in a terrible neighborhood and is listed for, let's say $15,000, doesn't mean you should make an offer of $5,000. Most likely your offer will not be accepted . You must be realistic if you want to get your offer accepted. Some tips that I can recommend to a would be investor to better their chances at getting an offer accepted is as follows:

1) Show proof of funds. This simply means going to your bank and asking for a letter that shows proof that you have enough money in the bank to purchase the property.

   If you're getting a loan to buy the house this letter should state exactly How much the bank will loan you and be signed by a bank official.

2) Remember, the bank will rather have cash. Cash offer's always trump a lenders letter offering to fmance the home. Sometimes the deal will fall apart because the bank will decide not to take a risk on fmancing the loan.

3) Be sure to inform the bank that you will like to include with your offer a earnest money check. (Although with

most banks you will be required to submit a earnest money check once Your offer is accepted) The more you put down the better. You won't lose this money. It will be deducted From the price of the home. If the deal doesn't go through, you will get the money back. Unless, you just walk away from the deal for no good reason. If that's the case, the bank can keep your earnest money as compensation for wasting their time.

4) Have your agent do some comparables (comps) for houses that are similar in price. Check to see what other similar homes in the same type condition have sold for in that same area you wish to invest in. This way you and your agent can decide on a price you both think is fair to offer the bank. Usually the banks will have already listed the property at a comparable price.

5) Get ready to go "highest and best". Because most of the time banks will wait to see if there are any other offer's for the property and If there are they will try to have the potential buyer's out-bid each other for the property. So always no exactly what your highest offer will be. I try to never go more than $1,100 above what I initially offered. Do not be dragged Into a bidding war. Just move on to the next property. There will be plenty more in tha hood.

6) Before submitting the offer you Should go back to the property and do a walk through. Be absolutely sure that this is the investment property for you. Are you ready to commit to the work, time, and money, it will take to re-hab it and make it livable again. Ask yourself "am I ready to be a landlord." Be certain that you want the property.

7) Read over the offer that your real estate agent is making carefully. Never let your agent Sign anything for you. Even though She's your agent you are ultimately responsible once you commit to that contract.

8) Always control the deal. Make sure your agent is experienced and professional. Remember, your agent is getting a commission from the deal for representing you. They work for you. You do not work for the agent, so do not ever let the agent slack in his/her duties.

9) Finally, do not get personally attached to the house. You may not get it.

When making offers on bank owned properties you never know if your offer will be the lucky one to get accepted. Sometimes a bank will accept the first offer that's submitted to them.

Sometimes I like to dig a little deep and fmd out the history of each bank owned property I may want to purchase. I usually go to the local County Auditor's web site to fmd out how much the bank purchased the property for at the Sheriffs sale? Then I compare that price to the price the bank is asking. Most of the time the bank will accept something between the original mortgage balance and the foreclosed sales price. If the property is under priced.

This is why it is so important to research the "comps" in the area. The market value usually set's the price. But if you're competing for "highest and best" sometimes the other bidder's offer a little more than list price. I, myself, have been involved in "highest and best" on several occasions and I have offered as little as $1.00 more, and as much as $1,500 more. When researching "comps" make sure that you also look at the last three months of similar sales in the neighborhood. Then look at pending sales. You'll want to try and fmd out what those accepted offer's were for.

Another thing that you can do is an analysis of some of the real estate owned (REO) agents in the area where you want to buy and research their pricing principles. They mostly always apply the same pricing principles to all their bank owned listings. If you don't know how, you can ask your agent to look up some bank owned listing agents on the MLS. Once you fmd an agent, run a search using that agents name to fmd the last three to six months of their listings. If most of their listings are selling for 5% over list price, then you need to offer 6% over list price. If the home is in a bad area of town and has been on the market for more than 30 days, and there has been no other offer's made on the property, you can most likely offer the bank less than what it is listed for and your offer will most likely be accepted.

Never ask the bank to make repairs or help pay for repairs or inspections. And if you request time to do an inspection try to get the inspection done as soon as possible because someone else could always submit another offer higher than yours. If you do find a problem during the inspection process, try to renegotiate only after your offer has been accepted. Sometimes the banks will pay for big repairs such as a hole in the roof. Also, remember cash offer's are a big negotiating tool. They are always more attractive than any other conventional fmance methods. Certainly, if you are bottom fishing in tha hood and come across some desperate soul who's about to their home to foreclosure a cash deal could help you bargain for some major discounting. Never forget that the more difficult a property is to fmance the more attractive an all cash offer is.

Once your agent has written up an offer and you've reviewed it she usually faxes it over to the listing agent that works for the bank. Be prepared to wait a day or two before you hear something back from the listing agent. If your agent submit's the offer on the weekend you'll have to wait until the regular work day begins because the banks REO department is closed on weekends and holiday's.

While I'm waiting to hear back from the bank I usually try to visualize how I'm going to fix the place up. I go over in my head where I wanna start first? Do I want to start upstairs or downstairs? Should I fix the outside appearance of the home first or should I start on the inside of the house? I always take picture's of the outside of the house, both back and front, and then the inside of the home. I walk through the property snapping shots of each room so that I can reflect back on it's condition. I try to envision how I would like the bathroom to look. Do I need to install a new tub, shower, toilet, or vanity? Or, should I just do a complete remodel in the bathroom? In most of these properties the conditions of the bathrooms are pretty bad. The home has probably been vacant for more than a year and vandals have by now stolen everything they could get their hands on. I take notes to remind me later of exactly what needs to be fixed or repaired. Then I do the same thing in the kitchen. Are the cabinets any good, or have they already been destroyed? Is there water damage under the sink? What about the plumbing? Is it still intact or has it been stolen too? Finally, are the floors in good condition.

I do all this looking and visualizing because I'm setting in motion the law of attraction. I'm already claiming this property as mine. I am putting in my mind how it's going to look once I fmish it. I can see myself already signing the paper's necessary to take possession of the property. I am simply thinking positive.

You see, from the first day I found the property I've set in motion a chain of events to help me acquire the property, and this is what the would be investor should do also. It's very simple if you want to get your offer accepted. Follow my steps and you will see that it will work for you too. Remember, the first thing I did when I made my offer was, I made sure I had cash to offer. Then, I walked through the home and pictured in my mind what it would look like fixed up. I aligned myself with a professional, experienced, real estate agent. I researched the property to determine what price to offer. I made sure to read over the offer carefully before having my agent submit it, and I fully controlled the entire deal. I saw the property that I wanted, I asked the entire universe to help me get the property, I fully believed I would have the property, and I waited to receive the property. Almost every single time when I've followed these steps my offer's were accepted and I got the property. The few times when my offer's were not accepted I simply took it as a sign that the property was not meant for me. Example: There was a nice brick 5-Unit brick apartment building that I really wanted. I thought it would make a great investment so I asked for it, believed I would get it, and waited to receive it. But somehow the deal fell through because there was another investor who wanted the building just as bad as I did. He submitted an offer above asking price and the bank asked us both for "highest and best". I submitted another offer thinking this time my offer would be the one that got accepted. But, it wasn't. This other investor wanted this property so bad that he submitted an offer almost $15,000 above the list price. I don't have to tell you, his offer was accepted and he took possession of the property. I was disappointed because I truly believed that this would have been a very profitable building, bringing in a stream of liquid income each month. What I didn't know was that this building had major unforseen problems waiting for the new owner. I later found out that this building had sewer problems, gas line issue's, and foundation problems. The cost to repair all the issue's were almost four times what the investor paid for this building. In the end, this guy had to sell the building for less than half of what he paid for it.

Moving along......Now that your offer has been accepted the bank will instruct their listing agent to take the home off the market. Because you will be paying with all cash there most likely will be no contingencies. Such as: Financing, inspections, and property appraisal. These are typical things that the bank will request when a buyer is using bank fmancing. As a investor, you should protect yourself at all times. This means having the property inspected by a licensed home inspector. You do not want to buy this property and then later fmd out that there are some major structural problems, or that the roof is about to collapse. Inspectors are easy to fmd, just ask you real estate agent or look in the phone book. Make sure the inspector you hire is aware of all the local city codes and regulations. Home inspectors usually only charge a few hundred dollars for a single family home, and about $350.00 for up to 4-Units.

Okay, the property is now in contract or escrow. Usually, if you are purchasing a bank owned property you will be purchasing it "as is" (like a used car) so barring minor details the waiting period to close should be very short. By now your agent will have gone through the process of forwarding over the contract and other necessary documents to a reputable Title Company to make sure there are no liens against the property. The property must have a clear title in order to be exchanged from one owner to the next.

Make sure that you have your contract and purchase agreement reviewed by your attorney. You will want to hire a lawyer that specializes in real estate law. This will save you a piece of mind and possibly lots of money should any legal issues ever come up later. Only after your attorney has carefully reviewed the contract should you then sign the purchase and sales agreement. This agreement will contain the exact details of the real estate purchase.

The Title Company will set a date and notify your agent when and where the closing is to take place. Normally, the closing will be held at the listing agents or the buyer's agents office, but sometimes it can be held at the title company's office. Since I buy a lot of properties out of state sometimes the title company will just overnight to me the documents to sign and have notarized and I will send them back. Although it really doesn't matter where the closing is held.

Before closing you should fmd a insurance company to arrange for coverage of your new property. If you're fmancing it through a bank the lender will require that you place insurance on the home. Sometimes they will even make you pay a one years insurance premium up front.

Cash buyer's are not required to place insurance on the property they are buying. However, I always keep insurance on my properties just in case something unforseen should happen. Since it will probably be vacant there's a chance someone could be squatting in it and thus damage can occur, or someone may accidently set it on fire, but no matter what, it's very important to keep the property insured. Home Owners Insurance is really not expensive. A typical small single family home will probably cost around $350-$450.00 a year, or around $45.00 a month.

I would like to strongly suggest that an investor obtain a home warranty and gas line warranty if at all possible. If you plan on living in the home at least a year you should try and obtain some kind of Home Warranty. Some insurance companies will not issue them to REO's but I know some that will. This insurance will cover a wide variety of things such as, appliances, plumbing, AC, heating, dishwasher,(if the home has one), and a number of other things that may be added. You should defmitely talk to your agent about this type of Home Warranty.

The Gas Line Warranty is especially important for those older properties in tha hood that have been sitting vacant for a number of years. This type of warranty once saved me more than $6,500 after I'd purchased an investment property that had a gas line that had ruptured. Actually, I have to thank my real estate agent because she is the one that suggested to me that I get this type
of warranty. Had I not obtained that gas line warranty I would've been out thousands of dollars.

Also, before the closing it will be a good idea to have all the utilities cut on and put into your name. This should include gas, water, and electric.

Now, it's time to close the deal.....

CLOSING THE DEAL

If you understand the closing process it will be exciting, but you must know how the process works.

Make sure you have the correct amount of money for the closing. You should have gone over the HUD Statement given to your agent by the title company. At the bottom of the HUD will be the fmal selling price after all calculations have been added or deducted.

Below are some of the fees that may affect the fmal sales price.

Real Estate Agent Commission: This is generally paid for by the seller (bank if it's a foreclosure), and both buyer and seller's agent will split this fee.

Loan Fees-Direct Loans: If your not paying cash for your new property then you will
need to obtain some type of a mortgage loan, and you will have fees to pay directly to the lender, and or loan originators.

Loan Origination Fee: Sometimes called a front-end charge to cover your lender's cost of fmancing and administrating the loan for you.

Points-Loan Discount: A one time charge by your lender to help you get a lower interest rate for your loan. If you pay for these points up front it will help you reduce your interest rate. Each point is 1% of the mortgage amount.

Appraisal Fees: Prior to approving you for a loan your bank or lender will hire an appraiser to determine the value of the property you wish to buy. If your asking for a $50,000 loan to purchase a house then the appraiser has to verify that it is indeed worth that amount.

Credit Report Fee: The lender has to run your credit to make sure you are credit worthy to buy a home. You'll want to have a high score to show that you're not a risk and that you'll be responsible for the loan. If you are paying cash this won't be necessary.

Inspection Fee: Again, if you are paying cash for this property you won't have to pay this fee.

Mortgage Insurance Fee: You only need this type of insurance ifyou're obtaining a loan. Cash buyer's will not need this msurance.

Mortgage Broker Fee: If you're using a mortgage broker to help you obtain a loan then you will have to pay for their services.

Yield Spread Premium (YSP): Tit-for-tat. Your lender will have to pay your mortgage broker a fee for fmding you, (The Borrower) and bringing the two of you together for the deal.

Signing all the paperwork will not take more than 20-30 minutes. While signing these documents the title agent will be briefly explaining to you each document as you go along. During this process the property will be transferred from the bank to you. Once you're finished signing everything, the property is yours!!

THE RE-HAB

Never be afraid of a real estate re-hab, no matter what size it is. Rather, big or small they are all the same. In this chapter I will explain just what you will need to do to complete an entire renovation from beginning to end. First, let's start with fmding you some good help.

For the initial clean-out I can usually fmd help at a few of the local city shelters. This is where you can fmd a few day laborer's to help with the clean-out. Most of the time I will go by the shelter's around 9:00am just after breakfast has been served. This is when the day laborer's will usually stand outside the shelter in a large group waiting for someone to come along and ask if anyone needs work for the day? I never pay more than minimum wage ($7.50) per hour no matter what their skill level may be. All I need is someone who can clean up and help me haul away some trash. Some of these day laborer's I can depend on for an entire day, and some will even last a week or two.

Once I'm done with the clean-out and the property is ready to be rehabbed I call my contractor. I cannot tell you how hard it is to fmd and then keep a good general contractor. You can look in the yellow pages or the back of the Sunday's Paper, but those contractor's who advertise in those big publications are usually higher than other handymen. Sometimes word of mouth is a much better way to locate a contractor. You may want to ask your real estate agent to recommend you to someone. I have a few contractor's that I use but my main one is "Keith". He can do anything to a house. There's nothing he can't fix. He can walk through a new property with me and tell me exactly what repairs we will need to make, and if we'll need to change any parts of the layout of the house. Even before I purchase a property I will have "Keith" come with me to look at the place to see if it's even worth me buying. If he tells me not to buy, I'm not buying. Other contractor's may see a place falling apart and know that it needs a lot of work and still try to convince me to buy the place, just so they will have some work. But, not "Keith". If he

1779-1781 E. Rich Street
My very first investment property

Seymour Ave. Duplex

508 Miller Ave. I told everyone that I know to
buy this property. I purchased it for only $2,200 and now before I've re-habbed it,

22nd Avenue house that I only paid $6,500 for. Today it's worth $34,000

Linwood Ave. Home sits right next to the home i grew up in.

One of my Wife's Investment Properties. It's a very nice brick cape code. She only had to do minor repairs on this home. A true diamond in the rough.

South Champion Ave. Building
After renovations

South Champion Ave. Building
Before renovations

4-Unit Apartment Building located at 1478 Forest St.

Side view of Forest St. Apartments
Purchashed for $52,000 now worth $120,000

899 Geers Ave. 4-unit Building
After renovations

899 Geers; before renovations

Middlehurst Property

Camden Ave. Property; paid $7,500 now worth $41,800

2866 Joyce Ave. Purchased for $1,750

1066 E.18TH Ave. Very nice Cape Code Paid $9,000 Currently valued at $50,000

Fairfield Ave. Home

Another Fairfield Ave. Home that I have just down the street from the other

Clinton Street Home

I like to call this one "The Mansion"
I got a good deal on this one.

"Misty Blues-Bar & Grill". One of or best investments. Sits on the corner of 5TH and St. Clair

Another one of my Wife's Investment properties. A half-double with tenants on both sides.

707 Seymour Ave. Before we re-habbed it.

707 Seymour after re-hab. Another good investment. We only paid $6,899 for the house and now it's worth $47,900

A home that also doubles as an office

One of our company work vans

Manor Road Home. The first home I purchased for myself.

Richardson Street home that I sold and made a nice investment off of.

A Birthday Present To Myself

Me standing in front of my home in Texas. I sold four of those cheap properties to buy this home.

Hard Work Pays Off!!

doesn't think the property is right for a rehab then I don't either.

Before we get more into how to start a rehab, lets first discuss how much to pay your contractor. Then we can talk a little about obtaining permits that allows you to even do the work.

As you and your contractor walk through the house take notes. You'll want to write down everything that he says needs to be fixed. Be sure not to leave anything out because it's very important that once you and your contractor agree on a price he doesn't come back later and create another job that will ad on more money. Only after you and your contractor have walked through the entire house and discussed each and every item that will need to be repaired can you start the negotiations of the price. Even if you use the same contractor for each property that you will re-hab. You should always remind the contractor that you will be getting more than one estimate for the work that needs to be done. Now, in the beginning I actually did go out and get several estimates but now that I know the business a whole lot better, I hardly ever get more than one because I can usually tell if it's a fair offer or not. Besides, "Keith" cannot tell me that he'll charge me $200.00 to paint a small room when I know damn well the going rate is only $50.00.

Most of the time, the way I draw up the contract is to offer a portion of the pay when my contractor starts the job, then when he's halfway through the job, and fmally once he's totally fmished with the job. Here is where you must again be careful because those fmal details that are to be made to a home is very important. Refer back to your list Has all the cracks been sealed? Has the door knobs been put on correctly?....So on and so on. I will talk a lot more about the fmal details later.

So you and your contractor both know exactly what work needs to be done to complete the re-hab. He tells you that for the entire job he will charge you $12,000 for labor and materials. You tell him "No...I will pay you $4,000 and I'll buy all the materials myself." Never trust your contractor to buy materials and bring you back a receipt, or tell you what he paid for the materials because most contractor's will never be totally honest with you. Remember, they're trying to get paid too. Sometimes the contractor will even be bold enough to accompany you to the hardware store and add extra supplies to your list that he needs to use on another job that he is doing for someone else. I would like to say to the reader that if you plan to be doing this real estate investment thing on a regular basis be sure to keep all of you extra leftover material to use on your next property.

Always try to negotiate the contractors price down as far as you can. Usually, if the contractor's hungry enough he'll accept a respectful counter offer. Remember, it will save you a lot of time and money if you can have your own day laborer's do the entire demolition and clean-out before the contractor's start their job.

Before we go on, I must talk a little about obtaining the necessary permits that will be required before you can start your re-hab. Building permits are not that expensive. They start at $50.00 and can go up to as high as $500.00 or more. Believe me when I say that it's a lot cheaper to go get those permits than it is to get caught working without one.

The fines for working without a permit can be ten times higher than what the permit would've cost had you just taken the time out to go down and apply for one. I have been hit with some of those fmes before and believe me I had to pay dearly. I think that the last time I got caught re-habbing without the proper permits, my fmes came up to a total of just over $7,500. That's no chump change!

Ok now, first lets begin with the exterior of the house. If you want to change the windows, and in some cities this goes for the roof too. You must get a permit. If you want to change the design of the porch or build a deck or any addition onto the house, you must first apply for a building permit.

Dealing with the interior is much more difficult. You will need permits for damn near everything. Changing lighting fixtures, repairing drywall (no matter how small the area), adding new electrical outlets. Any type of plumbing, heating and air conditioning, and to add or remove a wall. You must apply and get a permit before any work can be completed. I know it sounds like a lot but the city has to make a little extra money somehow, and this is just about the easiest way they could think of. Once you've gotten your permit and completed the repairs the city inspector will come out to your property to inspect and make sure that any repairs have been done the correct way. If the repairs are not done correctly you will be ordered to flx the problem and given a week to do so. If it's a serious problem the city inspector will shut your work site down completely until the repairs are fmished.

Now, back to the fun part. To do a cost effective re-hab you will have to most likely put in a new kitchen, bathroom, carpet, and paint the entire inside of the house with a fresh coat of paint. The outside appearance of the property must also be freshly made over to appear new or at least updated.

I like to start my re-hab off by cleaning the property out completely of any debris. Usually, there's no stove or refrigerator. The vandal's will have already taken those items to the scrap yard. Sometimes there's old furniture, trash, clothing, dead animals, and even feces that have been left behind.

Obviously, since there is no running water anyone that may have been living in the abandoned property has either used a bucket or a make shift comer somewhere in the home for a bathroom.

After I've cleaned the property out of debris and trash I rip out the carpet if there is any. Including the padding underneath. I check the walls and the ceilings for damage. If there's any holes or cracks I repair them. Then I prep the house for painting. I usually don't paint until all of my repairs have been completed. During the prep for painting I pull the hinges, switch plates, electrical outlet covers, door knobs, and window coverings if there are any. You'll want to walk through each room of the house to see just what you'll actually need. How many light fixtures, outlets, door knobs, switches, and hinges do you need? All these items should be replaced. Don't be cheap, and remember to buy light bulbs for each lighting fixture. I like to replace every light switch and every cover plate. If it's a very old house I like to also replace all the doors and hinges as well. You want your new property to be as new as possible. If you are going to try and sell the home you'll want the new owners to be impressed and if you are going to rent it out to Section 8, you'll want not only the potential Tenants but also the Section 8 Inspector to be impressed as well. It should cost you less than $75.00 to re-do each room. So, for a standard three bed room home that is $225.00. If I use a painter to do the painting I usually only pay them $50.00 per room, so add on another $150.00 and it will come out to be roughly $375.00 per room for each of the living area's.

Doing all this will make the house much more appealing to the new tenant or buyer.

Bathrooms: It's well worth it to do a complete rehab in the bathroom. Most of the time if the house is old and in a bad area the plumbing or other fixtures have not been upgraded, and there's probably water damage to the floor. Remove the tub, toilet, and sink. It will be a lot easier to replace the old flooring and to paint if these items are removed. While you have these things out you can replace the old plumbing. Wait to install the new toilet, tub, and vanity after you've painted and replaced the flooring.

Windows: Walk inside and outside the
home and check each window. Do they need replaced? Replacing windows can be expensive so if their not broken I would suggest just cleaning them and letting them stay. Adding blinds will spruce up any window.

Smoke Detectors: They save lives, and if you're renting they're required. Make sure to install a smoke detector on every level of the home including in the kitchen and basement (if there is a basement).

Kitchen: This is where you will earn the most money back from your investment. Usually, if the rest of the house is a mess than so is the kitchen. Kitchens are important. The first thing you should do is remove the existing cabinetry. Cabinets are not very expensive at your local outlet or Lowes. Also, try to get a nice counter-top to match your new cabinets. Make sure the plumbing in the kitchen is in working order, and you may want to consider adding in a cheap $49.00 garbage disposal. For the floor I would suggest a hard durable tile that can withstand a lot of traffic. If you're selling this new investment property or if you're going to rent it out, you will need to buy some good used Appliances. Every city in America has a store that sells used appliances so fmding some shouldn't be a problem. Also, you should try to stay away from the white appliances simply because they're much harder to keep clean. Black appliances are the best, but if you like the stainless steel look you can fmd the knock-offs that look like stainless steel at these used appliance stores also. These look-alikes are made of hard plastic and painted, then covered in a shellac to resemble steel. They actually look pretty nice. If you're going to be renting out the home I don't recommend installing a dishwasher. They are high maintenance and very expensive to repair. If you're adding a microwave I suggest that you have your contractor mount it above the stove up under a cabinet. Most new microwaves come with a built in blower already installed underneath them to catch any smoke.

Carpeting: The carpet gets installed last after everything has been fmished. You don't want to ever install carpets before your painting has been fmished. This could be very messy if the painter's accidentally spilled paint on your new carpet. So please make sure to wait before calling the installer's.

Front Of The House: This is where first impressions count the most. When the tenant's who are interested in renting come to see the house. Even though the house may be in the roughest part of town you'll still want it to out shine the rest of the homes on the block. The porch should be swept clean, and the mail box, door bell, house numbers, and porch light should all be new. Other outside cosmetics will include cutting the grass, trimming the shrubs and cutting back over grown trees. Planting flowers and watering the grass. You may want to paint the exterior of your new home also. You will want your new investment property to have curb appeal so walk across the street and take a good look at your new investment to make sure it's a place that you would want to live also, and if it's truly that nice then you've done your job.

There is no set price for how much it will cost to do a re-hab. Once you start investing in these types of properties you'll gain a decent amount of knowledge on pricing. Be sure to write down prices. Sinks, toilets, faucets, water heaters, door knobs, mailboxes, light bulbs, switches, cover plates, and paint will all be essential to your business needs. Don't forget to add the cost of big items such as tubs, cabinets, carpet, furnace, central air conditioning, and labor.

Rehabbing a house is not that hard to do. In fact, it's quite easy! If I can do it with only a few years of high school and some street smarts so can you. It certainly won't be easy in the beginning but if your persistent and have the desire, ambition, and motivation you can not only complete the rehab process but also create some sort of positive cash flow. People will always need a place to live. It doesn't matter if it's in the hood or out in the Suburbs

So now that your done with the re-hab it's time to begin the process of marketing the property to let people know that it's now "For Rent". So the next chapter will be about marketing and advertising your home, and creative ways to get tenants to want to move into your rental property. You're still not finished yet. There's a lot more that I need to tell you before you can go out on your own and attempt to become a successful real estate investor. So sit back, relax, and read on a little while longer. I'm almost done.

WHAT TO DO AFTER THE CLOSING

As soon as you leave that closing go straight to your new property and try your best to secure it. You might want to change the locks, and make sure to take the "For Sale" sign out of the yard. In a bad neighborhood you'll want to make the home look occupied, as if someone has already moved in. It's good to have already had the electricity turned on so that you can leave a noticeable light on inside the house, and if possible try to leave one on at the front porch. Sometimes I will go down to the " 99- Cent" store or "Family Dollar" and purchase some cheap blinds for the windows.

I do all this because I once brought a property and failed to secure it. I didn't even bother to go by and check on the place for more than a week and by then it was to late. Crack heads had moved in and were actually squatting in the place. I thought I would be able to just pick up a couple of my buddies and we'd just go by there and personally evict them all. That didn't happen. When we got there and attempted to put them out of the house they got belligerent, loud, and almost became physical with us. One of them told me that I couldn't put them out, nor were they going to leave voluntarily. So, I called the Police. It took them almost an hour to arrive and by then I had become very upset.

I introduced myself to the Officer's in a very professional manner and tried to explain to them that I had recently purchased the property and was simply trying to evict the squatter's from the premises. Well, to my surprise the Police informed me that I couldn't just put the squatter's out without first filing an eviction with the Courts. To make a long story short. The squatter's ended up staying there for another month rent free and when they finally did leave the place was trashed.

In a later chapter I will be talking more about the eviction process and what steps you'll need to take in order to do a legal eviction. You'll want to pay close attention to this chapter because you can be sued by the tenant if you don't do the eviction correctly.

If you don't have the money to immediately start the re-hab you should just secure the property the best way you can by either changing the locks, drilling screws into the front and back doors so no one can open them, or boarding up the entire home. This will prevent squatter's and Vandal's from trying to enter the property. Another thing that I sometimes use is a fake alarm system that sounds off if the front or back door is opened. You can buy these at "Home Depot" or "Lowes". If you have already placed blinds up at the windows and changed the locks, I guess the easiest, cheapest, deterrent, would be to just leave a radio playing all day and night so that anyone who comes to the door will think someone is staying in the place.

MARKETING AND RENTING THE PROPERTY

Before you start advertising your property for rent, you will need to first determine a few things. Such as, how much you'll be charging for rent, how long you will offer the tenant to lease for, will it be a fixed year lease or a month-to-month lease? What kind of security deposit will you collect or will you waive the security deposit? How many people will you allow to stay in your rental unit, and will you be allowing any pets?

Pets: I never allow pets. No matter who it is or what the case may be. True, in the beginning when I first started out in the real estate business I did allow my tenants to keep pets, but over and over again they would allow their pets to ruin my property. The pets would use the bathroom in the property and the tenants would sometimes not clean up the mess thoroughly after the pets. Especially, if the pets were kept down in the basement or another room in the house where the tenant didn't frequent regularly. Once the tenant moved out of the home I found out that it was extremely difficult to get out the awful smell left behind by the tenants pet. If you don't have the time, effort or the money to have the carpets cleaned or replaced, I would strongly advise against allowing any type of pets.

Security Deposit: As for a security deposit. Well, I like to ask for one because some tenants will destroy your property and not want to pay for any repairs. Security deposits usually covers most damage beyond normal wear and tear. Sometimes I will waive the security deposit if I'm running a move in special. When asked for a security deposit you'll want to ask for an equal amount to what you are charging for rent. So, if you're asking for $700.00 a month for rent you'll want to also ask for $700.00 for the security deposit.

How Many Tenants: When deciding on how many tenants I will allow, I always go by how big the home may be and how many bedrooms there are. Normally, you will want to allow no more than two people to each bedroom. If you are renting out a two bedroom house you can stipulate in the lease agreement that no more than four persons can occupy the premises and one guest at a time. You don't want to allow any tenant to move in their entire extended family.

Yearly Or Month-To-Month Lease: I never do month-to-month leases. It's to much of a hassle because you will have tenants coming and going. Moving in and out every couple of months. As soon as a tenant decides that they don't want to pay they will move out. Or, as soon as a tenant decides that they don't like you anymore because they asked you to fix or repair something, or maybe they even wanted you to allow them to be late on their rent and you don't move fast enough to the first request and say "no" to the second request. They will move out. No sir, I'm not having any of that. When I sign a lease it will be for at least a year, and if I can get someone to sign a lease for two-years that's even better. When I sign a lease I want to know that I will have a renter locked in for at least a year.

Amount Of Rent: To determine the amount of rent you should charge you will need to frrst know what rents are in your area. You cannot set your rent for more than what the market will stand for. If you're renting out to Section 8 the Housing Authority will let you no what you can get in any area of the city. Section 8 goes by what the rest of your neighborhood renter's are paying or should be paying. So if you don't want your rental Unit sitting empty make sure you have fair rental rates.

Finding The Right Tenants: In order to fmd the right tenants you'll have to develop different ways to advertise. The older traditional way was to place an ad in the classified section of the local newspaper or make up flyer's and pass them out around town. With today's new internet highway and all of it's social networks you really don't need to bother with spending a lot of money placing ads in the paper when you can advertise for free on the internet. Depending on where your property is located should help you determine where and how to place your ads. If the property is close to a college campus you can simply post some flyer's on their bulletin boards. Laundry Mats are also good places to advertise and so are some grocery stores, Welfare and Probation Offices, and the Volunteers Of America. These places are always trying to help needy people fmd places to live. Also, word of mouth seems to help out a lot. When it comes to the internet Facebook, Twitter, Myspace, and any real estate rental-specific websites are good too.

Hopefully, as I've suggested over and over throughout this book. You will choose to only rent out your investment properties to Section 8 Housing Clients. If you do this you can simply go down to the Metropolitan Housing Authority and place your property's address along with your name and phone number on their list of available homes and their clients who already have housing vouchers and are looking for a place to stay will automatically see your property on the available housing list and if they are interested they will call you to set up an appointment to view the property. Also, you can take a picture along with the address and your phone number and hang it on the bulletin board down at the Section 8 Office, so that tenants who are interested can see what the house looks like before they call you.

Make sure you are descriptive as possible about your property. You'll want to describe exactly what's inside. Example: Totally re- habbed 3-bedroom, 1 1/2 bath two story, single family home with new carpet and new appliances; asking $750.00 a month.

The proper advertising will expose you to lot of potential tenants. There will most likely be a number of persons calling to ask if they can fill out applications. Be careful about who you decide to choose. Make sure you check past history, criminal records, and references. The only way that your rental investment will make you any money long term is if you are a hands on landlord.

When you have fmally decided on a tenant you will want to meet the tenant at the property and do a fmal walk through. Check to make sure everything is in proper working order. Go over the rental agreement a final time and explain to the tenant all the important things that you want them to remember: Rent is due on time each month, no pets, they pay all utilities, no additional occupant's, no destruction of the property, no disorderly conduct, and any violation of the rules is subject to grounds for termination. When screening an applicant, make sure to ask for a copy of a picture I.D. or Drivers License. Make sure that same person is sitting in front of you.

If you are renting to someone with a Section 8 voucher the would be tenant will tum in his/her voucher and a Section 8 Inspector will call you to set up a day and time when they can come out to the property and meet with you to do a walk through inspection of the entire property. You must have everything in working order and all utilities must be turned on and working properly when the inspector arrives. If the Unit passes inspection you can allow the tenant to move in that day. If it doesn't pass inspection you will be given two weeks or maybe even a month to make the repairs. Once the Unit passes the inspection you will be called to come down to the Section 8 Office to sign the fmal contracts. Then you will start to receive a check each month.

At the very beginning, when a tenant moves into your property it would be a good idea to let the tenant know that they should purchase "renter's insurance". This type of insurance will cover damage to the tenants personal belongings should something unforseen happen. (A fire, break-in, or natural disater)

DEALING WITH TENANTS

When prospective tenants flrst come out to meet you and look at your property most will seem like very nice people. Some you can tell right off from a gut feeling that they ain't right. Those are the one's you never call back or follow-up on. Those are the one's that after showing them the rental unit you immediately tear up their rental application, and never call them again. Those tenant's that you do seem to like or have a good feeling about will always be the one's that can pass a background check. Their rental history has checked out, their criminal record is clean, they have good credit, a decent job, and make enough money to pay the rent. Most tenants are good people who always pay their rent on time, never causes any problems, and tries not to bother you unless it's totally necessary. But, you will always have some tenant's who are bound to be some kind of problem.

I've made thousands of dollars over the years dealing with some of the worst tenants, and I've made many thousand more dealing with good tenants.

The most common issue's with tenants are late rent, pet violations, and noise complaints. But you must remember that tenants have rights too, so as a landlord you will need to no specific laws dealing with tenants and enforcing their lease. The lease should be clear as to how and when rent is to be paid, if there will be late fees, and the things that are prohibited.

Although it is often times very possible to get a good tenant that doesn't cause problems and doesn't always complain and pays their rent on time every time. This is rare, and generally speaking bad tenants are also bad bill payer's. It's hard for some tenants to understand that most landlords are not rich, and most landlords desperately need to collect their rent money on time each month to pay their mortgage, insurance, property taxes, property manager, and maintenance. I guess it doesn't take much for a person to see that properties in bad areas (tha hood) often attract difficult tenants from all walks of life, with many different problems. You almost have to take on the role of a Social Worker to deal with some of the problems these tenants will bring to you, but as a landlord you don't have to like or dislike your tenants, or even have a personal relationship with them in order to collect your rent. I try to distance myself from the tenants altogether. However, as a landlord it may help to motivate the tenants to pay their rent on time if you are somewhat pleasant and on good terms with them. I must explain that there are two types of tenants: Those that pay and those that don't pay. Then you also have the tenants with the behavior issues, but generally the two go hand in hand anyway. In the property management part of my business I often have to deal with people and their emotions. Dealing with these tenants can be frustrating and even sometimes demanding on my time, sanity, and stress levels. Over and over again I have to remember that my tenants are not a nagging problem but instead the reason why I have this successful business. Although they may lie to me about why they can't pay their rent on time or hassle me about a maintenance issue, or even sometimes curse me out when I don't promptly return their calls. I still try my best to not get defensive, rude, or act arrogant, as if I'm better than them. I'm in a people business and I have to be diplomatic and no how to resolve their issues. You want your tenants to feel like they are just as important as you are. Tenants should no that no matter the size of their issue's or complaint, it still has merit. You have to empathize with them and thank them for bringing the issue to your attention and reassure the tenant that the issue will be taken care of promptly.

Now, I have to tell you that some tenants are just bad for you as a landlord, bad for the neighbors, and bad for your business. They don't pay rent or they simply pay late. They allow others to move into their rental unit who are not on the lease, they bring in pets that are not allowed, they sell drugs, and they keep up loud noise at all times of the night. Sometimes you want to just go over to the rental and kick them out!! But, you can't. Nope, don't even think about it. Tenants have rights too. So, for starter's you as the owner, investor, and landlord, better know the lease and the law. Be clear about it. When you draw up the lease you'd better specify in it if pets are allowed, when rent is to be paid, if there will be a late fee for late rent past a certain date, and what activities legal or non-legal are permitted on the property. Remember to include a catch-all "peace, quiet, and enjoyment" phrase that will cover anything that bothers other tenants or neighbors.

Furthermore, just because your tenant is not abiding by the terms of his/her lease doesn't mean you can just grab a few of your buddies and go over there and evict the tenant yourself. Once again, don't get it twisted. They have rights. You can't throw them out, or wait until they leave and lock them out, and you can't evict a tenant who has filed a complaint against you, because then it's considered retaliatory. Moreover, housing is protected by the Fair Housing Act, and the quickest way to get into trouble with the feds in this business is to single out someone or treat them differently.

As a landlord, the first thing you should do is to both call and send out a letter explaining to the tenant that he/she is violating the lease. Include a copy of the rental agreement highlighting the area's you're talking about. Normally, you'll be calling or sending out the letter for non-payment of rent, but if the phone calls and letter's haven't worked then I would say to immediately start the eviction process. In Ohio there is a three day notice that you have to give frrst. You must hand deliver or tape it to the front door of the residence telling the tenant to "pay rent or quit". Be sure that you know what your state allows. Some states allow three-days and other states may give the tenant up to 15 days to respond or move out before any action may be taken. Most states will even require that you show proof that the tenant has received the notice. I always cover myself by actually posing in front of the front door, next to the notice while holding a copy of that days local newspaper. This way the tenant can never say that they didn't receive the notice. Be sure to write on the notice the tenants full name and under the tenants name make sure to include "all other's" or "all parties". This is in case someone else who's not on the lease is now living in the residence and say's he/she didn't receive a notice and didn't know they had to move out. Remember, protect yourself at all times...

"CURE OR QUIT NOTICE"

For those's who pay their rent on time but has other issue's, like: Having pets, keeping up loud noise, disturbing other tenant's or the neighbors, or some kind of criminal behavior (like selling drugs). You can send out a notice to "cure or quit". In this letter you will explain to the tenant that you've became aware of the problem and that you are giving them a certain amount of time to fix the problem or face eviction for violating the terms of the lease. Again, make sure to include a copy of the lease highlighting the area's that are being violated by the tenant.

RENEWING THE LEASE

Some tenants you hope will never want to move out, and other's you can't wait to rid of. For those exceptionally good tenants that you want to keep, just before their lease is up you'll want to send them a letter letting them no what a pleasure it has been to have them stay in your rental property, and that you hope they will consider renewing the lease for another year. It would be a good idea if you included some kind of a gift card as a good gesture. I often times will send my best tenants a gift card for groceries from "Kroger" or "Wal-Mart" during the Holidays.

For those tenants from hell, you can notify them a few months in advance that you won't be renewing their lease and they will need to fmd somewhere else to live. So as not to incur any kind of property damage from an unhappy tenant, be sure to remind them that they will be getting their initial deposit check back if the property is in good shape. You never want a tenant to leave unhappy. There's just no telling what a unhappy soon to be ex-tenant will do to your property before they move out.

TOTALLY DESTROYING THE RENTAL PROPERTY

The worst part of an eviction process or a tenant moving out is that the tenant will sometimes trash or try to destroy the place before they move out. This is why it's a good idea to take picture's when your tenant's move in and when they move out of your rental units. Not all tenant's will leave a property trashed. Some tenants do it on purpose and others do it intentionally. For those that do it on purpose, well, they are just bad tenants who doesn't respect others or what belongs to others.

For those who leave a rental property trashed unintentionally it could be that they are just not very clean people who doesn't realize it. Or, they could just have poor hygiene or some bad ass kids who aren't properly supervised. But, it still doesn't give them a reason not to clean the place and return it as they found it.

Regular Repairs: A regular repair or minor repair is not in itself an emergency. General maintenance, including normal wear and tear are all the Owner/Landlords responsibility.

(Non-Emergency Repairs)
Carpet Cleaning
Carpet tearing or coming up
Water won't stop running
Cracked window
Toilet won't flush
One eye not working on stove
Refrigerator works but freezer doesn't

Emergency Repairs: By law you as the Owner/Landlord is responsible for any and all emergency repairs that's caused when something in the rental unit has broken and the health and safety of the tenant is in danger. As a landlord you should place emergency contact numbers in a noticeable place in your rental propertie(s). The emergency contacts should be: Yourself (the owner), Police, Fire, Ambulance, Plumber, Electrician, and HVAC person.

In some situations, if the property owner is not available and repairs must be made immediately to reduce personal damage, the tenant may have to call a repairman. If the tenant has called someone out to do a emergency repair, make sure you ask the tenant for copies of all paperwork related to the incident. Have the tenant instruct the repairman to bill you directly for the work done. If the tenant themselves has made repairs that are unnecessary or for their own personnel benefit, or for something that they knowingly caused, then it's not a true emergency.

(Emergency Repairs)
Broken Pipes (flooding)
Heating system is not working
Sewer system backed-up
Door locks not working
Tenant locked themselves out of Unit
Electric circuits not working
Refrigerator or Stove not working
Roof leaking
Basement flooding

COLLECTING RENTS

Collecting rent, on time, each month may be the hardest thing to do in this business. When you get into the real estate business your number one goal is to make money. This is done by collecting money each month from your rental properties, rather it be commercial or residential.

After all rents are collected you hope to make a profit, but the only way you can make any kind of profit is if you can collect all of the rent that is due. Some landlords can collect on time each month without having any problems, but for some landlords collecting rent is the hardest thing to do. There are a number of reasons why a landlord can't collect rents on time. A few are: Tenant's just won't pay, if there's two or more tenants living in the Unit one won't pay so the other doesn't feel they should pay either, or sometimes the tenant will say they're not paying because some repair was not made.

Although these situations come up from time to time and they are a headache to deal with, you should not be deterred from collecting your rent. There's a different way to deal with each tenant when they won't pay, and there are several things you can do to limit some collection issues.

Reminder Letter's: When a tenant first moves into your rental unit you want to make sure they understand that rent is due at the first of each month. Now, I'm sure that you would have by now discussed the rent and when it's supposed to be paid, when you and your tenant first signed the lease, but sometimes tenants will try you. So, it is in your best interest to make sure they get into the habit of paying their rent on time. I know your probably thinking to yourself that if your renting out your unit to a Section 8 tenant you have nothing to worry about, right? Wrong! Section 8 doesn't always pay the entire amount of the tenants rent. Sometimes they only pay a portion and the tenant will be responsible for paying the rest. The worst thing you can do, is to give a new tenant any kind of margin of time in paying their first months rent late. Because if you do, then what you are telling them is that it is okay to be late with their rent no matter what their excuse may be. This will only lead to them coming up with a new excuse each month in order to pay their rent late or not pay at all. You can never show signs of weakness when it comes to collecting your money.

Here's a suggestion. About a week before rent is due, send out a letter to all of your tenants and tell them that it's just a "friendly reminder" that rent is due at the first of each month, and that there will be a late fee assessed if rent is late. I usually inform the tenant that there is a $50.00 late fee if rent is paid after the 5th of the month.

You should remind the tenant how much rent is, and where to send it to. Again, remind them that the letter is just a friendly reminder. Do this each and every month or until you're comfortable enough that your tenant will be sending you the rent on time.

By getting your tenants in the habit of paying their rent on time, you will be also helping yourself achieve your profit objectives. Which is to create positive cash flow.

Make A Clear Policy For The Rent Payment: You only have one clear aim in the real estate investment business and that is to make money. A lot of it! So it is of paramount importance that you have a clear and specific policy on collecting your rents. Having a clear policy on collecting rent payments and making the process easy for your tenants, should help you as an investor ensure timely and complete collection of your rent money. Again, this should have been gone over in your lease with your new tenant. Never assume that your tenant will automatically know what to do with your rent money or you will be taking a chance of getting some later or non-payments. The following items should be reviewed with your tenants:

- What is included in the amount
- What period of time does the payment represent
- Who the check should be sent to
- Where the check should be sent
- When rent is due

- Instructions on lost checks
- What tenant should do if payment can't be made
- What the penalties are for late payments

Never confuse the tenant. Try to make the rent paying process as easy as possible. Make all payments for the same amount so there is never any confusion. Be sure to give clear instructions on where checks are to be mailed, picked up, or dropped off. Let tenants know if cash will be acceptable. Personally, I don't take personal checks because they tend to bounce, or I will have to wait several days for the checks to clear. I always inform my tenants to try their best to get a Postal Money Order from the Post Office because they are just like cash.

Don't Take Out Deductions From The Rent: One of the biggest mistakes you can make as a landlord is to allow tenants to deduct from their rent. For example: A repair needs to be made and you allow the tenant do fix it or you allow the tenant to call and hire someone to fix the problem, and instead of you paying the tenant or contractor directly, you tell the tenant to deduct it from the upcoming rent. This is a very bad deal, because it creates a situation where a tenant can easily dispute the amount owed to you, or even open the door for them to now start being short on further rent because of some made up repair that they've done without first consulting with you the owner. So it is a good idea if you as landlord handled all repairs yourself and paid for any services separately, not related to the rent.

Always Make Penalties Effective: Be sure to include in your lease a clause that explains the penalties if rent is paid late. The penalty should be a fme of a reasonable amount that increases everyday the tenant is late. I always make my penalty $50.00 if rent is paid after the 5th of the month. However, after the 5th I send out a notice to "pay rent or quit". Informing the tenant that if rent is not paid by a certain date I will file for an eviction.

It is very important that you discuss the penalties with your tenant(s) so they will be fully aware of the consequences of paying late. If your tenants are late you should try to speak with them to try and fmd out when they plan to pay or if at all they will pay? And, you must remind them of the fme they must pay for being late. Most of the time having a talk with the tenant will help with the collection process as well as getting you that late fee. You have to collect that fme. You cannot let it go or you will loose the leverage you created in the lease. Always try to collect the extra late fee whenever they fmally do pay the rent because this will have more of an immediate impact on them.

Remember, your efforts should only be aimed at collecting your rent on time every month. By making penalties and collecting them if warranted, will always help you get timely rent payments.

Hire Someone To Collect Your Rents: When it comes to money you have to handle it with care, because money is very delicate and has many different affects on ones life. Most people work very hard for their money and oftentimes they have a hard time letting it go, even if they owe it to somebody. By creating a delicate balance in your rent collection procedure, you can soften the impact to your tenants. One of the best ways to achieve this is to use someone else to collect your rent money every month. This is why I have a property manager. I use my property manager as sort of a buffer between me and my tenants. I don't want to ever have any kind of a personal relationship between me and my tenants.

A property manager can do a number of things for you and your business, such as: Make proactive calls, follow up on late payments, and review late charges. If tenants are more than five days late your property manager can follow up with a more serious call expressing their concern about late payments and reminding the tenant about the penalties for late payments. By using a property manager, you're also creating the image of a much bigger entity that is serious about collecting your money. You are also distancing yourself from the tenant so the tenant won't be easily assessable to you to make excuses as to why their rent is late. Using a property manager to collect your rent will keep you on better terms with your tenants and help ensure timely and complete payments.

Get To Know When Late Payments Are Most Likely: if you are renting to low income housing individuals, you will often times comes across tenants that go missing each month around the time rent is due. Or, sometimes tenants will disappear around the holi-day's. For example: Christmas break, Thanksgiving, Birthdays, and hot summer months. As a landlord it is very important to get a jump start on the holidays or any special occasions. If you're trying to collect rent on time, make every effort to contact your tenants well in advance and remind them that the rent is due soon, even if they have made plans not to be home around that time. Make sure to have your property manager suggest to the tenant that they make arrange-ments to pay the rent early or mail it, so as not to be late.

Threatening Legal Action: Personally, I don't like to take legal ac-tion against a tenant unless it is absolutely necessary. It's best to try and avoid the legal system to collect rent if at all possible. It takes to much time and energy to file the paper work and then appear in court. You will have to take off work and most likely you will have to pay all court cost. But, by all means use this most valuable tool if you absolutely have to.

After you've done everything that you possibly could to collect the rent from your tenant, do not hesitate to file a judgement with the court against your tenant for nonpayment. Your tenant will have to appear in court an explain to the judge why they did not pay you your rent, and you can file a lean against their current and future earnings. This will prevent the tenant from getting a loan or even a mortgage on a future home until the dispute with you is cleared. Using legal means is a good way to collect rent owed to you when your tenant won't pay. I will discuss the eviction process more in detail in the next chapter.

Finally, Don't Flaunt Your Wealth: Never pull up in your Big Beautiful Mercedes or BMW to collect your rent from your poor Sec-tion 8 Tenants. Don't rub your wealth in their faces. Your tenants will resent you and certainly won't feel bad about paying you or not paying you at all.

EVICTIONS

It doesn't matter how nice you are as a landlord or how well you maintain your property. There will come a time when you will have to go through the eviction process at least a few times in your career. Sometimes there comes a point when you will have to consider ending your landlord/tenant relationship. Even if that means no longer collecting rent from the tenant, because when you evict the tenant the property will have to sit empty for a short while until you can clean it up and do whatever repairs that may be needed in order to re-lease it.

Dealing with the eviction process in itself can be very stressful. It would be so much easier if we as landlords could just kick a tenant out for not paying their rent or for violating some other part of the lease, but we can't. Not without the tenant having his/her day in court. It's called "due-process". What this means is that a tenant must be served a "Notice To Vacate" and then given the opportunity to be heard before an officer of the court. You simply cannot terminate a tenancy without first following the correct laws of your state.

You can ftle an eviction on a tenant if they repeatedly violates the rules of the lease. For instance: Constantly not paying their rent, or each month paying their rent late, having a pet that specifically is not allowed in the lease, destroying the property, or selling drugs.

First, you should send a "Notice" asking the tenant to "cure or correct" the problem. If they haven't paid their rent, give them a chance to pay. If they have a pet, allow them time to fmd a new home for the animal. If they've damaged the property, give them time to fix it. If they are doing something illegal out of the property, give them time to stop whatever it is they are doing.

If your tenant agrees to fix the problems or decides not to and leaves then fine. Just let them go because you'll probably have more problems out of that same tenant later on down the road. This way you don't have to waste your time going to court and missing a full day of work.

Most of the time, after you've served notice on the tenant to vacate the premises and went down to file the "Motion for Eviction" with the court the tenant will not show up in court and the judge will grant you the eviction by default, but not all the time. Sometimes the tenant will show up in court and even convince the judge to give them another month or two to move out. During this time you will not get paid any of your rent.

This is why you should familiarize yourself with the eviction process from whatever state you have property in. If you want to win your case you're going to have to follow the eviction process correctly, because if you make one mistake the court may decide in the favor of the tenant, thus, allowing the tenant to turn around and sue you. Yes, this has happened to me once.

Lets looks at some of the steps you'll need to take to complete the eviction process.

Step 1: After the 5th of the month when You still haven't received a payment for rent. Tape a 3-day notice to "pay rent or quit" on The front door of the house. Remember, this 3-day notice is for three working days. No weekend, or holiday's.

Step 2: After the 3-days has passed you must then go down to the court And file a motion for eviction. The court will then send or try to hand deliver a copy of the motion to evict along with a Summons to appear before the Court to the tenant.

Step 3: In two or three weeks you and the tenant will appear in court and the judge will simply ask if rent has been paid? And, if you and the tenant both agree that it has not been paid the court will rule in your favor and instruct you to now pay for a "set-out".

Step 4: If you pay for a "set-out" the Sheriff Deputies will meet you out at the property and assist you with putting all of the tenants belongings out of your property.

This is basically all you have to do for an eviction. Never feel bad about doing a eviction because it's all about business. You want to make money and provide a better life for you and your family. No-matter, what the circumstances you cannot feel sorry for a tenant. I should also add here that it would be a bad idea to ever rent to friends or family. When I first started investing in real estate I made the awful mistake several times of renting to friends and family, only to be taken advantage of each time.

I think my family/friends both assumed that I would allow them some kind of leeway when it came to making their rent payments, and I was defmitely wrong to believe that just because they were family/friends they were going to be my model tenant's. How unrealistic was I to ever believe that! See, friends & family never feel like they have to come to you ahead of time to inform you that they'll be late with rent or possibly won't be making a rent payment for that month. They like to believe that because you now own a few investment properties you are somewhat wealthy. Some may even believe that you're now operating a charity in tha hood. So, I've had to evict both family member's as well as friends, and this put a terrible strain on my relationship with both of them.

When you're renting to someone who's close to you, they will always try you. They will constantly do whatever they want to in your property because they think you'll be cool with it.

The odds are never in your favor when you rent to friends or family. This is just like loaning them money, you'll sooner or later run the risk of damaging your relationship with them. So, if I can sum it up in 3-words it would be, don't-do-it!!!

CONCLUSION

Now that I've taught you how to play the game of real estate investing, I hope you will play it to win it. If you follow my lead and do as I've done it should be quite easy, but you can't let anything or anyone distract you from your goal. Which ultimately is to become fmancially secure.

Discipline will have to come into play somewhere along the line because you will now have a steady cash flow coming in each month and with that there will be much temptation to spend, spend, spend.

You must teach yourself to save for the next property. Don't spend on frivolous things or what you don't absolutely need right now. Spend only on what you will need later, and never do any kind of emotional spending on gifts for needy friends and family member's. Remember, "with wealth comes responsibility". If you're not responsible with the new wealth that you've worked so hard to achieve you'll lose it.

I've built my wealth up slowly adding one property at a time, so I've had time for my emotions and habits to develop and catch up to my wealth. For instance: Just like when someone hits the lottery for millions of dollars...their friends and family can bring many emotions into play, with their new investment idea's or always begging for some kind of charity, and the fallout from this can be destructive.

Don't be afraid to tell your friends and family "HELL NO"!!

Each month you'll want to put a little money away for the next investment property. If you've paid cash for the property and you now have it rented out, try your best to take half of the rent and split that half into two. Half will go for yearly taxes and the other half will go towards another property. You are now in the beginning stages of your real estate investing career so you should still be working at some kind of a regular job. If so, you'll also want to sacrifice a couple hundred dollars each month to put towards your next property. It may be hard in the beginning to actually learn or comprehend the art of real estate investing, and at times you may even want to give up but don't, because if you have taken the time out to read this book, that right there shows that you have the desire to want to succeed.

In the city that I'm from I was raised in one of the roughest parts of "tha hood". I had first hand experience with the criminal underworld. I knew "Pimps", "Hustlers", "Robbers" "Gang-Bangers" "Con-Men" and "Drug Dealers". I can tell you one thing, none of those people have a 40 lk, or a retirement plan to fall back on when they get older. But, I do...

I've found a business that I truly love and enjoy doing. I eat, sleep, and breath real estate. I do not have a desire to own more properties than I can handle at one time, but I do have a goal and that is to retire rich. With the properties I have now and with the ones that I will acquire in the near future. I will be able to sell them all before I'm 50-years old and retire still young enough to enjoy my Wife, children, grandchildren, and all that I've worked so hard for.

So let today be the first day of the beginning of the start of your new life as a successful real estate investor.

Start saving and doing the things that you need to do in order to get yourself familiar with the real estate business. Drive by some of those old houses that you see everyday in tha hood and try to imagine in your mind how nice those houses would be fixed up.

If you don't already have one. Get yourself a good Real Estate Agent and try to develop a good relationship with her. She can help you get your new team together so that when you are fmally ready, you can go straight to work.

Finally, think positive. Everyday tell yourself that you're going to be fmancially secure and free from all those bills piled up on the kitchen table. Act like you are successful, think like you're successful, talk like you're successful,and walk like you're successful and pretty soon you will be successful.